POEMS FROM
HOLLAND AND BELGIUM

TRANSLATIONS BY

C. J. Stevens

John Wade, Publisher
Phillips, Maine 04966

Poems from Holland and Belgium
Post World War II, Dutch and Flemish poetry
Translations by C. J. Stevens, American author

Library of Congress Catalog Card Number: 99-96820

ISBN # 1-882425-13-8 paperback

First Edition
Printed in the United States of America

ACKNOWLEDGMENTS

A line from "In the Park" by K. Schippers was used in the title of Sarah Provost's anthology of Dutch poetry "Carpet of Sparrows for young Readers" at *Nocturnal Canary Press*. Also included was the poem "Lullaby" by Nico J. Wilkeshuis.

A dozen or more pages in this gathering appeared in "Poems from the Lowland" as a *Small Pond Book* (Dutch and Flemish translations), No. 8, Winter 1966-1967.

Holmgangers Press in Alamo, California brought out the collection "Waterland: A Gathering from Holland." It was published with graphics illustrated by Eleanor Hjelvik Nelson in 1977.

Arts End Books of Newton, Massachusetts published a selection of translations called "From the Flemish of Gaston Burssens." This constituted issue number 11 of *Nostoc* magazine in 1982.

I thank James S. Holmes and William J. Smith for permission to include "Ballad of a General" by Paul Snoek which appeared in "Dutch Interiors" published by *Columbia University Press.*

These translations have appeared in the following jounals to which I give my thanks: *Abbey, Accent* (England), *Aesop's Feast Magazine, The Antigonish Review* (Canada), *Arx, Bardic Echoes, The Bitter Oleander, Black Sun, Bleb, Blue Unicorn, Caim, Caliban* (England), *Camels Coming, Cape Rock Quarterly, Cardinal, Charas, Chernozem, College Arts, Connecticut Fireside, Consumption, Continuum, Corduroy, El Corno Emplumado* (Mexico), *The Croupier, Cyclic Magazine, Driftwood East Quarterly, The Drunken Boat, Eleventh Finger* (England), *Encore, Entrails, Florida Education, Folio, Grande Ronde Review, Grist, Heirs, Illuminations, Image Magazine, Intrepid, Invisible City, Lemming,*

Maelstrom, Maguey, The Milk Quarterly, The Miscellany, The Modularist Review, Mojo Navigator, Moving On, New, New Laurel Review, The New Renaissance, The Old Red Kimono, Olive Dachshund (England), *Open Places, Outlet, Out of Sight, The Other, Other Voices, The Penny Dreadful, Pierian Spring, Podium, Poet Lore, Poetry Dial, Pot Hooks and Hangers, Quartet, Quill Magazine* (England), *Quoin, Radix, Red Cedar Review, Resurgence* (England), *Riding West* (England), *Salted In The Shell, Second Aeon, South, South and West, South Dakota Review, Sou'wester, Stone Country, Talisman, Tautara, Tejas, Titmouse, Tombstone Nine, Trace, Tulsa Poetry Quarterly, Unicorn, Voices International, The Washington and Jefferson Literary Journal, Webster Review, Wendigo, Wetlands, Word, Zahir,* and *Ziggurat.*

Further acknowledgments are made to the following publishers for permission to use these translations: *A. Manteau N.V., EM Querido's Uitgeverij N.V.,* and *Uitgeverij Heideland.*

CONTENTS

FROM THE DUTCH

FROM THE FLEMISH

Preface

Dutch poetry had its beginnings in the twelfth century and reached a peak five hundred years later with a group of poets whose reputations were well-established within Holland but little known in neighboring countries because of language insularity. This national achievement, however, was short-lived: it was followed by two centuries of conservative and church-going verses that paralyzed the force needed to spark another revival. Only in the 1880s did a refreshed generation of Dutch poets, mostly influenced by the English Romantics, rise to the forefront. But these voices were not rebellious enough to shift emphasis from a parson's kind of poetry laced with monotonous scansions.

Such conventionalism discouraged individuality. In the mid-thirties, Dutch poet Cees Buddingh translated W. H. Auden and Garcia Lorca for literary reviews and every editor in Holland called such poetry a madness. It wasn't until after the German occupation of World War II that a new generation of writers came into their own. Poets began to ignore the iambic line and sonnet and allowed themselves a greater freedom in imagery. But this experimentation met with fierce resistance by critics and readers who were crowding the corners of traditional poetry. Literary warfare sparked controversy during the fifties, and in the embroilment more avant-garde magazines and anthologies gave better exposure to poets striving to find their individual voices.

In Flanders, that slice of Belgium bordering Holland where Dutch is spoken, the climate was entirely different. "Modern poetry" invaded Belgium earlier because the country had not remained neutral as had Holland during World War I. Influences in guises of German Expressionism and French writing that broke some molds of tradition prior to the conflict were being established. Flemish poets, such as Gaston Burssens in the forties (he died in 1965) and Paul Snoek (1933-1981) in the sixties, were instrumental in shaping postwar writing in Flanders. Over the years, Flemish in the South and Dutch in the North have gone their linguistic ways, even though many Flemish writers are published by Dutch presses.

A newfound exuberance that could absorb the elements of Surrealism, Imagism, Futurism, Vorticism, and Dadaism was unleashed finally in the late fifties and early sixties. The centuries of Calvinism were shoved aside rudely as experimental magazines, such as *Gard Sivik* and *Barbarber*, did much to democratize creativity. Poets now could go their own way unselfconsciously—enough so that the most noticeable characteristic found in Lowland poetry by the seventies was its diversity.

Such individualism created a chain of rivulets trickling in every direction and away from the mainstream. Dutch and Flemish poets were now free to strut brazenly as post World War II nations became global economic villages. The barriers were flattened and a clearer view of what others were doing came into focus as communications began the flirtatious dance toward the silicone chip. T. S. Eliot's *The Wasteland*—which was looked upon as a craziness at the time it was first published—and Allen Ginsberg's *Howl* were now poems that Dutch critics took seriously. Both the traditional and experimental approaches were totally acceptable. A number of young poets in Holland found themselves returning to rhymes, metrical norms, and some made regular use of the sonnet, a form that took longer to regain limited popularity in Flanders. Dutch poet Lucebert dazzled readers with an experimental sonnet: "I/me/me/I//I/me/me/I//I/me/mine//I/me/mine." Anything was possible; everything *did* happen.

This selection is formatted to give a view of what has been going on in Holland and Belgium without anthology proportions and biographical decorations. I first became acquainted with Dutch and Flemish poetry while living in the Netherlands during the sixties—one year in Apeldoorn and six months in Valkenberg near Maastricht. Translation was one way of experiencing the creativity around me while writing my own things. Over the years, many of these poems appeared in journals, and this book is a final selection. I hope readers will share some of the excitement and pleasure I had in collecting them.

FROM THE DUTCH

Remco Campert

IMAGINE

Imagine: we were snowbound
The food was almost gone
The radio broken, shoes leaked
Notebooks full of memories
We burned for a scanty warmth.

And the flag we had somewhere
Hidden we used as
A blanket of course. There was
Absolutely no hope
Not even hope for hope. Still

I was not unhappy because
Death was coupled with
So many statements of love
From you to me, me to you
That I could not

Achieve unhappiness. Time
Was lacking. There were always
Breasts to kiss, eyes
To reveal, and when we were tired
We slept and dreamt of

President Roosevelt

K. Schippers

IN THE PARK

Not the policeman with the bicycle
who stands near the blue teahouse
not the man by the river
what he sees I can't tell
not the woman with the baby carriage
who is coming in my direction
it's the old man on the bench
and I on the other bench
we both see
see how my carpet of bread crumbs
becomes a carpet of sparrows

Sake Helder

POEM

Each morning I shovel snow
on the mirror
of a soaped face
the early morning frost
alum
dictates this poem to me
with little pinpricks
of a new lotion
armed with more courage
than my belt can hold
I walk into the day
glistening with good intentions

Ben Wolken

DAWN

I find linen light
around your head
but it is not called day
under your pale eyelids

spiders of light
crawl over your shoulder
and how can I awake
I who have not slept

the paths begin to live
behind your stranded hands
a fisherman goes on his way
how far behind your bent back

wouldn't it be better
to turn off the lamp
it has outlived itself
in this ill-born light

Ellen Warmond

METAMORPHOSIS

We knew
that time mercilessly consumes
like a whole army
of hungry caterpillars

but not
that it would suddenly reveal itself
to this moment
full of marvelous butterflies

Warmond

CLEAR

Wait without wishes
do not move only
breathe attentively

think clearly and patiently of
emptiness

see how time gets thinner and becomes
a clean skeleton
of reality

Warmond

LATER

Later is
a long and soft
or a small and sharp
sorrow

this we have known
for a lifetime

but not now

Warmond

BETTER

Rather than writing or speaking
to desert language
to become a speechless animal
to groan significantly
from pain fear or pleasure

better to think in vowels
growling yelping bleating
living with a letterless tongue
the heart a gong
the circulation a sonata.

Warmond

HURRY

Call this moment a burning flower
a sweet-smelling torch or if needs be
simply love
but hurry before it withers
like a bridal bouquet on a nail
above a stripped bed

hurry before it lapses
into the dreams of a drunken demon

a clubfooted dervish
who has forgotten his magic

Warmond

EN ROUTE

My eyes choose from the passing landscape
what later my brain may digest
as an ancient image myth or memory

what lies behind me closes itself as a circle
of which I no longer play the center
the unseen suddenly feels itself unwanted

trees and mountains wait with decaying
until I have passed and I have seen them standing

Warmond

NOVEMBER BLUES

From a warm sleep we evening
through the nightly nobody's dark
driven here
in the I-celled I-light
of the morning

this is a fluttering birdwingmorning
in an almost unrepeatable autumn

so let us try
to pick up the day carefully
to say: look the morning is
an open hand and can you
read the future?

Warmond

SMALL BARBARISM

When he had found the courage
to let his hand grow
in accordance with the secret wishes of muscles
no longer beggar palm
no longer the parrying fist
but claw

he sharpened his nails on
granite and shook
his arms awake from
the hammock of the past

struck

and struck as always
in emptiness.

Warmond

VIEW

What can be seen:
a hole in a hole
the body barely fills
its own space

we are too much fear
who shall understand whom?
we are too much human
who says anything?

we look at each other
we know nothing

Warmond

THE SCHOOL SATCHEL SEEN AT CLOSE QUARTERS

Three dry elderly Englishmen
all descendants from a branch of Leicester
climb in mountain shoes to the hotel terrace
as if they wished to mount a parasol
seat themselves carefully in their creased skins
(But fairy tales stand cooling on the tea tray
even mermaids swim here with snorkels)

and behind them the widow
from Göttingen admires the panorama
that enlarges her view of the handsome
sunburned Spanish pimp in the bathing trunks
envelops him in a fat German daydream
full of sehnsucht leidenschaft and whipped cream

and already in all the Spanish churches
the people begin to pray for their salvation
an aging corpulent Lorelei
makes the whalebones of her swimsuit sing

Warmond

EVENING

Seconds walk angrily backwards
the day has toppled out of time

I become as silent as a beach
on a winter's night   I become
as empty as a fire-gutted
house   life stands further
away from me than I can tell

lay your face in your hands
and try to imagine this

Leo Ross

HOLLAND

Lowlands

this pasture needs
a red roof;
the wet swan, under the wordless sun,
paddles through the water weeds and stops by the willows
that stand in a row all their hanging lives;
the farmwife is reading in the mock sunshine
of the tiny house; in the kitchen, porridge
is on the stove.

This is the water land where Flora
picks buttercups.

Truth is taken like an old cow
out of the pond; wandering Pegasus
is strolling through the marshes and has relinquished
the last thoughts of an abyss.

The make-believe lava in a painter's cloud
disappears.

Dear drunken landscape of Holland,
I can look at you fully without drunkenness.

Ross

THE OLD MAN

Then comes the day that I shall not get up
my ribs rattle on loose screws
the lid of my heart hangs loosely
my last yawn crunches like a door
my teeth chatter in the glass
my wig drops from the nail
the canary growls and the goldfish
lustily joins in the song
the cat moves barking into her box
does the sun shoot ravens over the dunes?
god shall love, I am going to sleep

Ross

AUX AURORAS

Around us the sea
a lonely airport for fishes

Sometimes I laughed at something you had said
at a word with an afterglow

In the mast-high light
the rolling moonlight, so strange, so naked,
and so wet, your eyes drew
a green track, probed a slowly
graying image of stars

I watched how the great sail
of the sky caught the light
like wind, and waveringly began
to swell, I felt that
the city
ceased its tossing

And we took leave

Pierre Kemp

POEM

There I go again with a cone
full of stars on my head
I once walked much straighter,
but then I still believed
that brides could come
and take those stars
for their veils, but those dreams
are now wasted.
Little has been left me
but this body without giving
and receiving, besides
my eyes can see no more brides.

J. Bernlef

ON THE WAY TO THE BLUE MOUNTAINS

In the past—judging at least from
old paintings—one walked
after breakfast
straight to his own loneliness.

You know those blue mountains in the haze
there are no roads to them
but they can still be reached.

I sometimes think about this
in the morning when I breathe on a mirror.

Bernlef

HAPPY LIVING

The behind of a mandrill
seems to say: hurrah—where I end
the world begins

I, on the other hand, am so differently naked
as on an evening at the beach   like rolling stones
the palms of my hands bend and wave

wave and bend
and my voice seems to come from a rock
and I compare and listen and sometimes
I'm orderly as a child with his toys
my room will be neat
I will draw a boundary that constantly vanishes

how well I could use a noisy behind
I could turn to the world
my flashy end—it would be a happier life.

Bernlef

THE DEAD LIZARD

His death is a handsome pose
at the bottom of the well
magnified by the water:
lying on his back with curled paws
he carries his graceful autograph
up to the curve of his tail,
his hat and umbrella have decorously
been removed from view.
So dies a gentleman, a lizard.

The ticking of my watch almost pushes
through the motionless mirror of water.

Bernlef

VANISHING POEM

Where do I find the word
that hasn't died in a poem?
I shall look for it as a
child looks for a self-made kite
that trembles and falls and rises
a kite that slowly lifts in the sky
and at last vanishes.

Nico J. Wilkeshuis

MORNING ON THE YSSEL

maybe this is
the key to the secret of time and space
unfortunately the philosophers are still asleep
they dream of love or dream of traveling
this moment there is no one in the world
but a fisherman standing on the bank
now and then he pulls up a small cloud of mist
a brave little ship
distant and invisible
is puffing through the gray universe
the church bell: six blows of cotton wool
they fall like pillows on the world

now the whistling window cleaner is coming
to wipe the blurred windows
of the new day

Wilkeshuis

LULLABY

between us
stands a piano
the tones are paper boats
cryboats blue
laughboats yellow
and boats of desire
that take you through the mist
then they blow
as fragments through the rainy world
where the moon is sad
and lights blink in a wet street
go to sleep
and count the boats in your dream

Piet Calis

HELPLESSNESS

poems go to bed in the evening
and go to sleep
go to sleep soon

but words
words are lovers without hands
and the heart of a word is too heavy
for the night to carry

words are always awake

Calis

AWAKENING

this night a floating flower
you a laughing sand-star
a fireball in the sky

I played hide-and-seek with your eyes
and I slept on the beach of your skin
and your hair sang a top tune, a hymn
your hands a song of the sea

come come
and I danced in delight between your breasts
skated over the ice of your hips
grew ivy along your legs
I kissed your body of sun

but when I slowly woke this morning
I knew
I was still a man
in the caravan of time
I knew
our speaking was a house without silence
I knew
these were the stuffed birds of love

W. J. van der Molen

HORSES

Around a table of grass
they stand close together
under the lamps of the trees.

They are so home-loving, almost afraid
of the wind and the dew that is coming.
Their tails hold back the rain;
they only go out together.

van der Molen

DUSK

You laugh almost audibly
as you walk next to me through the evening
with the world at our feet.

The wind is on its knees
listening to the high rain
and the exulting birds.

I see you with my conscience
and my thoughts hear you
busy behind reality.

van der Molen

FAREWELL

I pin a butterfly on your blouse,
which you can look at
when I have left you.

On the nails of your fingertips
I have placed ten eggs,
to laugh at if necessary.

I have arranged the wings of unknown birds
in the vase of your eyes,
like empty paper flowers of silence.

And on the backs of your two hands
I lay packages of lavender seeds,
oil for your hair and feet.

And around you, in the house where you live,
I shall let the mirrors gently kneel,
so that the farewell will almost be a feast.

Bert Voeten

COCKTAIL PARTY

With a clown's face
I open the door
with long teeth
I eat words
of others
my own words
jump like
jockeys over
holes of silence
joy and sorrow
come from the
periphery of
my voice and
dance on their toes
ridicule turns
somersaults—
a night animal
howls in my throat.

Voeten

IN MEMORIAM MATRIS

For my father

I
I was still a sailor
in blue pants from the sea
and my father was captain
my father had four harpoons
and a pipe with black tobacco
and boots that reached his knees
and I tobacco-chewed licorice and spat
and pulled in the mooring cables.
We sailed on big ships
loudly honking through the streets
we sailed along the boulevards
and I was first on land.
We walked through long halls
over brown shiny floors
and it smelled like the sea but different
I felt myself getting seasick.

II
Women with long skirts
ships with dull hulls
sailed past and white
tables on rubber wheels
were pushed into side halls.
Everywhere there were glass
doors and light signals
and talking as if under water
I felt myself getting seasick.
"Come here," said my mother.

34

Voeten

She lay in a big white ship
her hands over the railings.
"Why don't you laugh?" I asked
"I wish I had a ship like that
I would sail to America
let's catch whales!"
But she did not want to my mother
I said: "If you don't play
I'll never take you out sailing again."
"Perhaps tomorrow," said my mother
but tomorrow did not know her.

III
Tomorrow was sun and milkbread
and tea that got cold and men
with black coats and letters
with black borders and questions
"Will we sail again today?"
And the hand with the white handkerchief
the hand on my head the hands
over the rails of chairs
the still hand next to the plate.
Tomorrow was playing outside
in a different street
before windows with rolling blinds
and tomorrow was going shopping
and the looks in women's eyes
and speaking more softly than usual
father who kept coughing
the smell of camphor and flowers
in a room that remained dark
a room I did not know.

Voeten

IV
Tomorrow was sailing after all
along the sunny boulevards
and I was first on land
I who ran into the garden
with my pockets full of pebbles.
Tomorrow was grass and gravel paths
and asters and apple trees
the black pants of my father
a woman with a white cap;
tomorrow the yellow of the shed
a sheet a door that creaked
tomorrow my mother sleeping
in a narrow ship my mother
sleeping backwards—
"Doesn't she want to play anymore?"
"Perhaps tomorrow," said my father
but tomorrow did not know her
as I had known her.

M. Mok

FOR YOU

For you I still listen to time:
immovable feet in the blue
fire of the evening, unmoved mouths
in which the pain has softened to sadness.

For you I still listen to fear:
the life that cannot confess its dream,
and eye to eye with forgetfulness
fights for postponement.

Mok

DRAWING BOOK

Daily there are wonders. My father comes
every evening out of the world space
into the warm house, clears his throat
and lets loose his worries. My mother covers
them with a handful of words. That starts
the human in me to move:
faces become stars, arms reach
from above to below through the cool
blue of another night, every word has
a resonance that makes me shiver.
And later, when I plunge to my sleep,
at the end of my thoughts, I see again
the drawing book of a hidden hand.

Fritz de Blauw

TRAVELING THROUGH

during a day they came
during a night they left
they have known the peace of the evening
also
they ate war in the morning
have suffered their love for the last time
since the storms
they have vanished in the night
after
I believe
having lived only one day
like a slave.

Peter Berger

POEM

When silent and naked
you lay next to me
and it was autumn and
smoke tasted of nuts

and of long-haired wind
I bent
over your strangely
shining face

and there moved in your eyes
the laughing of the young
child that breathlessly still
lives in this poem

Paul ten Hoopen

WOMAN IN AN INSTITUTION

I see her years older:
a still life too weary to exist.
She fusses about corks on the water,
weekend boats that sail around the corner;
and when I want to ask something
about the small tragedy of her forty years,
she tries in vain to chase away the animals
that graze on her narrow shoulders,
that empty her breasts, before the winds
sadly toy with her dead hair.

Yvonne Kaul

HERE ON THIS DUNE

Here on this dune
People who have awakened
Complete the action
I see for the first time:
The birds are exhausted
The plants have all died
And the woman who forces
Her child to greater speed
Is right when she says:
A dead bird is dirty
Throw it away.

Clara Eggink

THE TENDERNESS THAT IS SILENCE

Softly, on the moonlight strings there rustles a tree finger.
The wing beat of the owl is a thought of sound.
His call doesn't unload the silence.
Far, far to the west the surf sighs.
The earth lifts itself with dampness and fruitfulness.
And two,
          whom tenderness has turned almost to mist, say:
Hush, we love.
Softly, there is the first grass covered by snow.
A shy dark animal slides over the glimmering white
and threatens soundlessly.
The moon stands wild and tottering in the wind.
The sea lifts itself in a long dark swelling.
And two,
who from their warm dread have turned almost
                              to glass, say:
Hush, we must die.

M. Vasalis

HOMECOMING OF THE CHILDREN

Like big flowers they come from the blue dark.
Under the freshness of the evening air
with which their hair and cheeks
are lightly draped,
they are so warm. Caught
by the strong grasp of their soft arms,
I see the full shadowless love
in the depths of their deep-transparent eyes.
Still unmixed with the human pity;
pity that comes later—and has reasons and boundaries.

Vasalis

THE WINTER and my love are gone.
There is a blackbird on the roof,
his throat moves and his beak trembles
as if he were talking to himself.

He listens: from a distant tree
comes the ricochet of pebbles
a spark-rain of desire
so loud, so clear, and so afraid.

The blackbird plunges with a cry
of wildness into the stiff wind.
And I can hardly bear it:
my spring and my love are gone.

P. M. Croiset

TWO POEMS

I PLAY KING OEDIPUS

tenderness my mother never showed me
I cannot remember a kiss
but before she died she said
she loved me
because I looked like my father

INSTINCT

the seagulls stand
with their faces to the storm

I can imagine them turned around

I'm surprised
I still have arms
and legs

Phia Baruch

MY MEANING

My meaning
is a red dream
that will not touch earth

The voice
of broken glass
deep in the water
far under sand

My meaning
is a bird
with slippery feet
and hungry.

V. Valentin

TAUT LANDSCAPE

The profiles of bicycles stand out sharply
on each side of the drawbridge:
a steep colossus, and a thin file
of stream creeps past the indolent mud.

And on the country road the disheveled souls;
the high saddles place their bodies on display.
They travel with the wind that lumps their shirts,
the bunglers of a busy industry.

The landscape threatens to tear at the seams:
with zigzag stitches, a bird sews up
the ditches with web-thin, silver threads.

The tautness seems to slacken momentarily.
The drawbridge has collapsed under its burden,
and is kneeling with a broken spine.

J. de Gast

BEN-AMAI

Ben-Amai walks unwashed through the
streets of his city
with his bird on a string
he talks through his hair
and compares the women of
the opposite side
to the women on his side
(most of the women he likes—
particularly those on the opposite side)
his bird chirps with pleasure and
releases the string
Ben-Amai grips the back of his head
and swings with his left leg
only his eyes
still live in the city

Mea Strand

RODRIGUEZ

He is back
rodriguez
red and shaggy
with bare feet
quickly each cobblestone
kisses a toe
see there steps
rodriguez
big black see
the oiled knee
the loose sweater
embraces his neck
a black left eye
passes above me
like a painted man
on a vase
rodriguez
rodriguez is loose

Hans Andreus

IN MY SOLITUDE

Not now.
Happiness has folded its wings,
sits amazed in a corner,
doesn't go up the street anymore,
into the air anymore.
Not now.
No time for restlessness
to see behind a wall,
around the corner of a street,
through the empty glass,
under the world—
to look at the nucleus of the sun
and those of the many systems
and back. Now is the crossing.
Now is no time for confrontation.
Leave me. Now is alone.

J. Greshoff

THE TENANT

All that was given me yesterday
To live with
For a moment
Is taken away
Today
Or tomorrow
Without reason:
My worries
My watch (Antoine frères Besancon)
My green woolen dressing gown
My dreams
My eyes, nose and ears
Paintings, statues
Ties
Walking sticks
The fresh green for old goats
My complete Henry James
And, quite in its completeness, between Schelde and Eems,
That dear piece of ground
Where once my cradle was found.
All that I paid for bloodily
Is taken away
And the neighbors' things too:
Possessions go up in smoke.

Even the things we were proud of
The famous soul strings
Stretched tightly and characteristically
And certainly worthwhile,

Greshoff

A beggar threw them in the canal.

All my furniture and organs
All my laughter and my tears
This city and nature
I have, expensively
Only for rent.

In a little while
Hein will come here
As coachman
With a whip and a high hat
And say to our maid
Who opens:
"It's for the old man,
For Jan,
He knows about it.
Luggage and clothes superfluous
He will not even need a toothbrush..."

And there we go!

Hans Keller

POEM

To pray is to beat language out of lead
and to let loose the word like a red balloon
to pray is to fly joyously over the sea
and to drink blue beer at two in the morning
to pray is to drive the yellow-dwarf car
in the country lane
and on Sunday to take pictures of your voice
to pray is to look at trains together
to say late in the evening:

look we are still here
let us be happy
our feet move
our hands move
we can make and break
let us be happy
we are still here

that is why to pray is more than
making god laugh

Charlotte Keuning

HITCHHIKING

We hurry star-swift through the night
over silver canals of car lights
along flames of white tree trunks

In the clock it is still dark
nothing chews time
the fiction god escapes on all fours
into the book
he loses his top hat on the way
I hurry forward to my origin
over the approaching end

J. J. Veenhuysen

DES NUITS D'ARLES

in me
and around me
the earth is black silver
old ships
of a thousand words
sail solemnly by

there is a beginning
of green starfish
of evening-singing streets
frightened birds
travel slowly over the river
and in the armed grass
invisible crickets bury
a buzzing secret

restless
and snorting sounds
the breath of bulls
behind the wind
of insane red
lies the waiting plain

Han Foppe

FUGUE FOR LIDY

this is a time of weeping willows
I said
you nodded and sighed yes
this is the time when the clouds
lean over towards the unknown
a time of empty hands
this is a time of weeping willows
I said
and you were crying

Hans Warren

HERON

Small silent bird
bowed at the water's edge
the winter bounces gray from your eyes
ebb and flood push whispering
through endless creeks
a brittle reed breaks
bird that half listens
to the tossing of a distant fish
and half frozen with lack
buries his beak in his feathers

Luitzen Visser

POEM

I have felt the night downy with rain
and have watched in a landscape gray with sleep

I know of voices behind the curtains of night

and of the whispered riddle
of gravel under a late sudden footstep

I know the scarce breath
of hours longer than their shadows

they are things one meets with yes and amen
but stiffly and without satisfaction

Visser

À LA DIOGENES

time is
the gloomy account of the rain

and I see myself walking looking for someone
who is like an ordinary day full of flowers
and drenched by the sun

Alfred Kossmann

ARIA OF THE GROWN-UP

When she comes home too late
Smelling of air and street
I search in my strict reception
Between care and punishment
The sublime balance
And we dance on points of rope
I anger, she repentance
I hardness, she asking for help
I forgiveness, she thankfulness
Till we in subtle glow
Blue of eye, red of cheek
Make up, bow and leave
Last stance in the pas de deux
Last glance in the warm dance
Which she will later, more lightly
Lovingly dance with her dolls
And who with me?

Guillaume van der Graft

WHILE WRITING

While writing I had fallen asleep
while writing I woke up in the night
because words stood bleating outside
under the open window where I lay.

Who had driven them there together?
Was it hunger or was it the wind?
They stood in a beginning rain
dead silent and shivering on the gravel.

Then I took them with me upstairs,
the big pane of the mirror blurred.
I had never known how one
half asleep carries words up the stairs.

But in the morning when I awoke
they had gone and the door was open.
The sun was shining high and dry; there were
birds laughing in the woods.

van der Graft

SELDOM DOES ONE SUCCEED

Seldom does one succeed in writing
in such a simple way
that each word is a child
breathing in the
bed of the language
under the blanket of the poem.
Writing in such a way isn't easy.
Sometimes one wakes up
the small child
who asks for something impossible.
Give him something; anything
you don't understand.
Then turn on the lights,
and sit for a long time on the
edge of the language reading
what he says
word for word
hand in hand.

Nico Verhoeven

ON THE HELMETS

On the helmets of thunderheads
there romps an amorous spring sun.
The city builds itself in bird flight.
The café terraces become an El Dorado again
with their parasols and light activity.
The whole day is an album of photos;
in the evening one turns the pages and sighs.
In the evening one thinks of the coming day,
of the evening with the embezzled light,
of the evening itself; a fence of worries
twilights the book. One closes it.

From the Flemish

Jos Vandeloo

SPANISH CAPRICCIO

I forgot your name
was it Anita
or Carmen
or just simply Maria?

there are so many
stars
planets
and women

so many
Anitas
Carmens
and Marias

many atoms
form one body
many women
form many memories

was your name Anita
or Carmen
or just simply Maria?
I forgot your name
but not your body.

Vandeloo

CHILD

In the train
a child asks
what is a cow
and what is a horse
what is water and fire
what is the sky
the sun
dew and mist

there are a thousand questions
and ten thousand answers

in the train
I think
what is a child

there is one question
and one answer
wonder.

Vandeloo

AND LONELY AS MY WORD

This is the speaking of the sun
a soft barking full of pleasure
a wagtailed word

the breath of space
the number on the almanac
the wild sleep of young years
the smell of wood and fire
inflammable are our dry days

listen carefully then
to the impossible voices
head to the side like a king
the soft voice of the prophet
proclaims harsh lies
the sun alone is faithful
and lonely as my word

Vandeloo

ONE/TWO

1.
I tore the coat of my word feelings
into two pieces
in a burst of charity
one for the beggar on the left
the other for the vagabond on the right
now both pieces lie on the street
in the hollow throat of the wind
and I am naked and cold

2.
my feet in the low tide
of fear
between my toes is
the grass of unrest
and who mows the grass
mows my feet.

Vandeloo

AND NO ONE

I have brought the high priests
of boredom
before an altar
on which naked young women
will slowly be sacrificed

the high priests will
do their duty smilingly
or what they call their duty
and later in innocence
will wash their hands

and no one tomorrow
can read the fingerprints
on the face
of time

Vandeloo

UNCORRECTED THOUGHT

each hour
time pecks
a grain of corn
from the barn
of my life

perhaps my granary is
nearly full
that doesn't help
time is patient.

Vandeloo

A LOWLAND ANECDOTE

A man bought a piece of fallow land
and worked night and day to make it fertile.

He weeded and sowed and a few months later
the man harvested a beautiful crop.

The priest came to him and said: "With the
help of God you achieved some fine results."

"You have a point there," answered the man. "But
when God had to do it by himself, it wasn't much."

Jos Vandeloo

AND THE OLD MAN

And the old man
rainface
and his voice
liquid lead
he speaks softly
melted words
freed birds
fly around his head
and his firefly
eyes dance
in heaps of hope
with his rainface
hopeless old man
and his soft birds

Gaston Burssens

SNOW

Sparrows chirp loudly
cars hum louder
trams ring loudest

Through the centuries stars are
symbols of ideal desire
snowballs star open
snow is white on black
camouflage

when the king is in Nice
the court jester throws snowballs
the footmen ride in sleighs
with the members of the parliament

The sparrows fly forlornly
and chirp loudly
the barometer points to changeable
snow is camouflage
on Christmas night no baby will be born
in a garage

Burssens

POEM

Sometimes when the sun shines through your windows
—and all things are only sometimes—
through the clear glass of your laughter
which happens only sometimes

Sometimes when the light of your thin thoughts
circles in bright curls
and above endless layers
a somber flame dances before your eyes

then your hand is filled with emptiness
your heart has slept to weariness

and no one knows if you still will hear
the sobs and the games of the young monkeys
of your impatience

Burssens

TO THE MEMORY OF MADELEINE

I have put my fear to rhyme
with many an oath as a request
to myself and all my friends,
searching what I search and what is intangible,
yet lay for the grasping,
the laugh, the belly laugh of the nirvana
as delusion of my resistance.
Then I put my fear to rhyme
for centuries less than a day,
for days less than the plural
of a simple song
and for the singular that was less than
getting used to a sorrow.
I can, I could have known
—of course I, I didn't know it—
the poison was only intended for me,
a woman's bite is multiplied
and then honored
in one snake, the one from paradise,
whether I believe it or not.

Burssens

DESPAIR

Along the sloping plain of the senses
the moon once pushed her stark light

And whoever ventured on this plain
has weighed himself
and lighter than the rays
has bent his own fragility

And this is good
The rays have not been violated
and the starkness of the light remains inviolate
Only the iron of your senses has been twisted
and has been weighed and found too light

Burssens

PROVERB

The electronic eye now aims
at every movement.
Its beam which should be purple
shines green on my face.

Purple and green are as poisonous as the questions:
What used to stop me from sleeping?
Why are my temples grayer
and wiser?

I know the beam pierces my field of vision
as if my eyes
must search implicitly the wisdom in certain things,
that drip from the rain in the drop of stars
—when one must either pump or drown—
close to the electronic eye of the needle
through which my camel will soon have to pass.

Burssens

QUARREL

Your cheeks are chilly and moist is your hair
and your coat drips with rain.
We walk resentfully together
against the tugging wind.

We do not speak the words now,
the paltry foolish words;
instead, the storm sings its song
in sneering chords.

We do not ask for kisses now.
We walk cold and aimless;
you do not even open your umbrella;
we are numb to everything.

Burssens

MORE MODERATO

Nightly there hangs
a gentleness that is not tangible
far from the nightly groping of our eyes
probing the darkness

For our gentleness was never unending
and God be praised never without sin
the dear lies and the true ones stood
entangled like hopeless seaweed
became a truth—one that crawled
within the seaweed of hopeless hope

Where green hope and black seaweed
are disentangled and rigid
for reasons of greater embellishment

Where all hope was dispelled with gentleness
we are patients of a diseased life
now and forever given up as useless

Burssens

TO MYSELF

This is, so be it, the last note
that I shall, will, can, play
in the last life that I live,
on the last keys of my body.
An instrument hard as a safe
from which I have squandered the craziest pennies,
from which I have pulverized the most expensive spiderwebs.
The dust has stuck to my bones
and will be buried with me.
The worms will not eat it,
the poison is only intended for me.
Each beautiful song decorates itself with a conclusion,
as each conclusion decorates itself with a prayer after eating,
and that this end, now or never,
must be called beginning.

Paul de Vree

AFFLICTION

tell the splintered cupboard
and the broken wall
of the never-allayed burden
of the never-recovered hour.

tell the blinding flight
in the absurdity of azure:
the bodiless light delight
of the childish-earlier fire.

go tell it, tell,
trust to the nightly silence:
how the older, later game
missed the spring of april.

de Vree

THE WRITING OF POETRY

the poem is always to break
the previously achieved connection
to speak out with relief
constantly in different song
of tone and magic sign
in the undiscovered land:
to revenge oneself creatively
on the provoking nothing.

Andries Poppe

DUALITY

I stand with my heart in one hand
and my head in the other hand,
and to the rhythm of the wind I sway
back and forth between dream and intellect.
No matter how much I try,
I never remain balanced:
seen from the left, I'm a number;
considered from the right, I'm a poem.
My skull is full of perceptions
that my inclinations can't touch;
and what my heart tells my lips
my head has never understood.

Pol le Roy

DREAM

And all night I saw, looking speechlessly at each other
two trees: one full of stars, one full of darkness

and all night I saw, lonely and mourning for each other
two hands pearl-silent with white sorrow

from all the windows the death-fear of your eyes called
and birds turned restlessly from themselves

then I confessed to you and you laughed strangely and unmoved
and not a single morning clung to your fingers.

le Roy

AUTUMN

Listen, rumbling through the mountain pass, on the drab horizon
the carriages of the wind, and the capsized keels
dance into the mist and the thundering water.

A glow washes over and lingers with a strange ache
around hills that no longer stand in this life;
over a field of glittering rubies
I watch the sterile beauty of my dreams go.

le Roy

CALLED

The door, a lined-up fall in the light. Bleeding, one lands
on the cellar floor. The steps, the days, the years, the
dead animals on the walls of childhood. Then: the tedium
of the poles, the columns, the temples, the pulse-glass glow
of coldness. But each side street cries raucously of hidden
and forbidden wonder: the jungle, the night, the dark river
of freedom, the swaying reptiles of the blood.

Palladian, oh woman and so bewilderingly the double-shell of
all pearls, all jellyfish, all light and your healing and
your corroding poison in all the veins of the earth. The
seeping gold of misdeed, the silent bed, the warm honey of
sleep and the breaking, robbing, stumbling hands.

Make a human out of all this.

Who must see, know, go, love, be loved. And must know himself
when the door of death is slammed shut. And must go on.

le Roy

POEM

a hand had only
dry branches left
and the dark wind
had only the candlelight
of the day left and startled wings
then fell the snow
the land became a petrified chrysanthemum
and death took a last
look in the mirror and strolled
into its somber enchantment

le Roy

READINESS

Someone walks down the rocky path of the evening.
In vain he looks for a house. This approaching
thunderstorm permits no morning anymore.
My castle blows open. The lightning conjures
with a distant bird. Past the horizon there
already begins the broken endurance of death.
I shudder at this paradise. I shudder at the
script that blazes in the black plants. Without
mercy, without grief, I turn away—tanned in
timeless acid.

The stones of the moon carry my steps. In between
flows the gray fluid that comes from the dead.
Happiness belief delight mercy, it is hailing
unwinged creatures in my face turned towards
the hidden law. To the very mirrors of emptiness.
Lightning upon lightning increases my distance
and my range.

I rest in my dissolved strength.

Now I shudder only at what is to come. Great
and inhuman with certainty. Unapproachable for
myself I shall put fists on the land of those
who failed. Hard and high in this absorbing blind
right: to be.

le Roy

IN MEMORY

Embittered and verbose. A night of whoring. What does one add to the sloping shade of the years? The treasures of your childhood acquire shadows and become frayed or crumble away. You grow in poverty and in knowledge of poverty and in the illness of your poverty.

You become great and stately. You become a pillar. Temple even. Stone and damnation. A holy place for cockroaches and parasites. A tourist point. Until the frosty sheet of death covers everything. Your portrait is disgustingly fingered and wept upon. But you are finally safe in your sleep. Hallowed with the wisdom of death.

Clem Schouwenaars

SAGA

I come up from the earth
concave rock
with water and dead leaves
birds and boys
drink from my bowl

when moonlight
lay at my forehead
a child was conceived
in my shadow
I am the wailing wall for women
and the nostalgia of bodies

I carry runic writing on my back
and beetles in my green skin
no prominent man will dare
build a city from my rock

for the saga is told
of feasts around my altar
and the screams of virgins dancing
naked and without shame
in the fire of family trees
and letters of nobility

Schouwenaars

THE DYING

we have arrived at this point
without blessing without silver without poetry
who shall widen the earth's desk

for centuries we have waited for the four trumpets
in the morning around the hut of clouds

we have arrived at the rock
ask the blind man in the wind its name
the ferryman or the cardinal
who calls this silent-rock or end-rock
or a beginning

at this boundary all that remains
is a diving into the milky way
in a mock-realm without regret
and ready for sacrifice

Paul Snoek

AIR CASTLE

I wish, before I change
into a rock, an ant
or a poppy,
to become the creator
of an air castle

I shall cut the roof
out of wrapping paper,
fold the rooms
from damp newspapers
and on the walls of sheet music
I shall paint laughing faces
behind windows
with metal ink.
In my castle shall live
doves of old silver.

I shall, before I change
into a stone, an animal
or a creeping plant,
become the creator
of an air castle,
for I have
the soft hands
of an inventor.

Snoek

A GIANT

A giant knows himself.
He looks for a girl sweet as a rabbit
to juggle in and out
of the big hat of his heart.

But a giant is too lofty for a girl,
and she is too blue with submissiveness.

The race of giants is dying out. A pity,
for he can stretch open his eyes
like dough and can make his muscles play
like snakes tiresomely.

A giant is crazy about ice cream
and honey from fat bumblebees;
bees that make the lungs of the rock buzz
like dwarfs in a watertight jail.

A giant knows what he wants.

Snoek

SUMMONING COURAGE

I dreamed of gentle lagoons,
of forested skies full of palms,
and of uncharted bays—
overpopulated with women.

These alone can save me:
the calm of a drainage canal,
the quiet of the acquiescent sea,
my posthumous work in bottles.

Why should I still shiver
when I hear my national anthem?

Snoek

A SWIMMER IS A HORSEMAN

Swimming is licentiously sleeping in sprawling water,
is loving with each still usable pore,
is to be endlessly free and to triumph within.

And swimming is touching loneliness with fingers,
is arms and legs telling ancient secrets
to the all-comprehending water.

One becomes the creator embracing creations,
and in the water one can never be quite alone
and yet be lonely.

Snoek

BALLAD OF A GENERAL

Red from glory and fat from defeats
washing himself with steaming water
the general stands in front of the window
of his only room.

The women of his career
cut at two sides,
for his stomach is hairy
with the kisses of swords.

Despondently the general lets
his manly breasts, acquired
during a campaign in Europe,
hang resignedly.

Wet from water and red from Waterloo,
the general stands in front of
the only window of his room
drying himself with the tricolor.

Snoek

AFTERNOON IN AUGUST

Little girls with star-tail hair
play rainbows with a bouncing ball
against a geranium wall
by the back roads of the universe.

Boys blow on the harmonica of the day
and shout behind the hoops of planets
along the dam of the Milky Way.

And mothers with cauliflowers in their hands
talk long with the greengrocer
about the weather.

At this hour
there are no fathers
on earth.

Snoek

WHEN MAN WAS STILL GREEN-YELLOW

When man was still green-yellow
a walking plant on feet
of turned-over sunflowers
with a melon for a head
his words were pieces of sun,
little smiles.

Not everything swims in pompous water.
Colors became dangerous
and I who wanted to find the earth
like a starfish
found a pulverized pearl.

For me the stars
have become much older.
The earth continues to play its day-and-night game.
I have remained
like the first rolling stone,
a man full of holes.

Snoek

POEM

Her wax hand, thin
as a water scorpion,
closed and opened, up and down
like a tame butterfly
in a tame flower.

She sowed
three silent buttons
on the garment of love:
one of silence, one of sorrow,
and one of mother-of-pearl.

As if her big mouth
had something else to say;
silently an unknown
whispered word
stayed on her lips,
as if she were touched
by the stone of wisdom.

Adriaan de Roover

POEM

long long after the wind
fled from the hides of animals
fled from the fish-scale leaves
the trees were still dizzy
I am cold in the forest
now I want to wash my words
with evening moss and dark water
my words have become dirty
living in the mouths of thousands

Books by C. J. Stevens

Poetry
Beginnings and Other Poems
Circling at the Chain's Length
Hang-Ups
Selected Poems

Biography
Lawrence at Tregerthen (D. H. Lawrence in Cornwall)
The Cornish Nightmare (D. H. Lawrence)

History and Adventure
The Next Bend in the River (Gold Mining in Maine)
Maine Mining Adventures
The Buried Treasures of Maine

Translations
Poems From Holland and Belgium

Animal Behavior
One Day With a Goat Herd

Fiction
The Folks From Greeley's Mill
Confessions